DEATH DID US PART

CAROLYN S. SCHRADER

STOKE Publishing

ISBN 978-1-988675-46-6
STOKE Publishing

DISCLAIMER
This book is not intended as a substitute for the medical advice of
physicians/psychologists. The reader should regularly consult with medical
professionals in matters relating to his/her health and particularly with respect to
any symptoms that may require diagnosis or medical attention.

For bulk purchases for support groups and healing circles, please contact the author
directly at:
carolyn@carolynschrader.net
carolynschrader.net

Dedication

I dedicate this book to my beautiful Daughter-in-law, Violeta, who has believed in me, read every manuscript and encouraged me from the very beginning. To my Son and Granddaughters, Matt, Erika and Erin, who supported me through this whole journey. To my VBFF Jan Moore, who has sent me daily texts of encouragement since my husband passed away. To my publisher, Jennifer Sparks, who makes magic happen and has made it possible for me to finally realize my dream of becoming an author. To my editor, Beth Jarrell who performed her magic with the expertise of profound knowledge and experience. I am very blessed!

Contents

Preface

Grief is a complex and powerful emotion. Each loss I share with you in this story provides a very real glimpse of my experience with grief. Though the stories I share here may be short, in truth, each could be a novel of its own. However, for the sake of length of *Death Did Us Part*, I have given only a small selection of my losses. Each synopsis shows the different scenarios of what I experienced and what was expected of me from others when a loved one died.

Introduction

This book is written from my personal experiences with loss and grief. Each loss could be a book all its own, and one day I may very well write about each one. All my reactions and experiences are my own experiences; they are in no way meant to infer how you or anyone should go through loss and grief. Every person experiences these things on their own terms, according to their belief system, value system and experiences in their personal lives.

Most of you have some experience with grief, the loss of someone or something that has affected your life deeply. I believe that every component of grief brings us to another level of our human experience on our short journeys on earth. In the coming chapters I will be sharing my own experience with the shock, pain, and the levels of grief that I have gone through and how it has affected my life and what grief has taught me. My experiences with grief may be very different from yours or may be very similar. We, as humans, often walk side by side in moments of grief, veering off from time to time to walk our own personal path. There are times we must walk alone for the healing to begin and do our best to understand the plight that has been brought into our lives and onto our very soul.

As you read my words, it is my hope that you will find grief has many components to it which includes benefits as well as pain. Before you experience it or go through your own walk with grief, you cannot know how you will react or recover and get through it. Know first of all that you need never to be alone in grief unless you choose to be. Everyone we meet, know and don't know has experienced grief on many different levels.

We will always live alongside of our grief, we are never apart from it. However, we may very well have a space in our heart and soul where we can allow our grief to rest knowing it will come to the forefront of our emotions when called upon. Each time we give our grief the rightful recognition and emotion it deserves, the impact will most often soften the edges to some degree and allow us to better understand that grief can be the intricate bridge to learning how to live a more aware life.

Each book that has been written, concerning grief, provides the opportunity of giving its reader another perspective about grief, hope and the understanding that they are not alone in what they are feeling and experiencing. When I went through my own grief, I learned the hard way how to maneuver through the emotional and bewildered states I would find myself in. The directions my feelings would take me did not always fit into the original 5 to 7 stages of grief.

It is my hope that my experiences and knowledge will help with the maneuvering through the process of loss and grief, and give a different perspective to some of the issues that may be faced. I also want to shed light and give some preparation for that which we do not know until we have gone through it. For all that I have written and all that you will read, there will always be more. More ways of experiencing loss, more ways to grieve, and more ways to get through your grief. As you read my story, experience, knowledge and guidance, please remember that no one person has all of the answers on getting through grief. Know that you are never alone with your grief and when grief is coming down hard and feels unrelenting, it is ok, and it may very well be necessary, to ask for help to get through. I highly encourage you to ask for whatever help you feel you need to manage the grief you find yourself with.

Going through grief is an extremely personal experience. Grief over the loss of a loved one is not temporary. No one gets over grief, we can only get through it. However, as we go through grief it is just as important to practice gratitude and remember, write and speak about the things we are grateful for about the one we have lost.

What is Grief?

One of the many definitions of grief is from The Free Dictionary – https://www.thefreedictionary.com

- Grief is a deep mental anguish arising from bereavement
- Grief is intense sorrow caused by the loss of a loved one
- A keen mental suffering or distress over loss, sharp sorrow, painful regret
- No matter the type of grief we experience, the path of going through it is hardly ever smooth.

ONE

Our Story

─────────────

Hi, allow me to introduce myself. I am Carolyn Schrader. I was born in Missouri and lived in Washington, Alaska, New Hampshire and now, I am living in a perpetual vacation land known as California. I have been blessed with a varied career. I was a licensed Hairstylist for over 50 years. I was fortunate enough to be an on-air radio announcer with my husband as well as a Continuity Director for the whole of my husband's radio career. I sold radio advertising and was the commercial copy writer for the radio stations I worked for. My career in working with the public took me to one of my most cherished positions I have held, The Armed Services YMCA of Alaska, (ASYMCA), where I began as an office manager moving up the ranks to became the CFO, and Deputy Director. While working at the ASYMCA I became known as "Mom" from the enlisted troops to the Generals and because of this gifted title I was asked to write a column for a military newspaper. My column was titled "Ask Mom" and most of my writings and advice was tailored to our military and their families. I retired from that position to work with the Alaska National Guard as Coordinator for the Military Family Assistance Center. While working with the families of our deployed service members I became a

Certified Professional Life, Grief and NLP Coach with an Associates of Psychology from the University of Phoenix. The duties I performed were that of Teacher and Trainer of Life Skills. My certifications cover grief, crisis, suicide and emergency preparedness. My present career is that of a Writer, Blogger, Trainer for emergency preparedness, Certified Professional Life and Grief Coach. My experiences with grief have not only been on a personal level but on a professional level helping others understand their losses and maneuver through their grief. All of my experiences have been painful, powerful and life changing. I have had to cry, cuss, walk out my fears and learn the hard way through many losses brought about from death. On a personal basis, I have gone through the death of two beautiful children, my husband, grandparents, parents, aunts, uncles, cousins, siblings, many extended family members, friends and pets. I have experienced personal health losses, jobs, homes, dreams, possibilities, relationships and at times the loss of who I was.

I well know what shock, pain, anguish, disbelief and grief feels like and how it can change us. My husband and I lost our little seven-teen-and-a-half-month-old twin boys in a horrendously horrible accidental carbon monoxide poisoning. My husband suddenly and unexpectedly passed away. My heart and soul will never be healed and I will feel the pain and miss them all to my last breath. There are still times when I am asked about our little guys that I cannot get through their story without breaking down and other times when I can talk about them and relate their little antics with a smile. This is not uncommon for those who have lost children. I have learned the importance of taking deep breaths and thinking of the joy they brought us as opposed to the pain, and extreme sadness their death brought to us.

My husband and I were together for 46 years and married for 44 of those years. One week after our 44th wedding anniversary, my husband literally dropped dead on one of his favorite golf courses. He always said that when he had to go, he only wanted to go two ways, in his sleep or playing golf. Therefore, as so many tend to say, he went the way he wanted and he went doing what he loved. While this is true, there are many times when I absolutely hate that cliché about death and want to scream that I'm pretty damn sure he did not want to go at all! Hearing someone say he died doing what he loved does not bring anyone comfort and never will.

Since my husband is actually the catalyst for me writing about grief and much of what it entails allow me to introduce you to who he was and a little of our story. I met my husband, one month after I turned 21, at a country bar and dance hall. I was out with several co-workers and on one of the bands breaks he came sauntering over to ask me to dance. He was all cowboy that evening and had my attention from his first "howdy". After dancing together for the rest of the evening it was time to go home and at that point he asked me for my phone number. I was being quite confident in myself and responded flippantly that he did not know me well enough to have my phone number therefore, he could call me at work and we could have lunch. I later learned that he found that response quite comical and it peaked his curiosity but what he did not know was that I had already fallen for him. He called and we went to lunch. During our lunch I found out he was active duty military, seven years older than me, had been married twice and had three children, two from his first marriage and one from his second. This was a big wow for me and I knew instantly this was not going to go well when I told my family, specifically my dad. Sadly, our dating, engagement and wedding was fraught with disapproval, turmoil and disappoint-ment. This is also a book of its own therefore I am only giving a brief explanation of who we were. About six months after we met he said he needed to get a part-time job to add income to his mili-tary pay. I told him he should be a country radio announcer since he seemed to know every country song and singer on the radio at that time plus, he had a killer sexy voice. He was sure he would need to have more training than knowing the country songs, however, I convinced him that all they could do was say no! One afternoon as we drove through town I saw the number one country radio station and got him to pull over and go in and talk to them. My attitude was, might as well begin at the top. After about 45 minutes he came out and of course I started asking what happened, what did they say, will they train him or does he have to go to school for being a radio announcer, to which he just looked at me, started the car and pulled out into traffic. At that point I am thinking uh oh this is not good. You see my attitude was always go for the gusto, why not, they can only say no and if they do then move on and find another way, and that was not necessarily his way of thinking. After we had driven a couple miles down the freeway he glanced over at me shook his head and said, "I start tomorrow night". Did I gloat? Absolutely and this began his and our country music announcing career. Because he taught survival and evasion for the military he was told he had to use a different name to work in a public forum. He and another announcer came up with using part of his middle name and a name off of the control board at the station. He became known as Jim Robbins. He started his radio career in Spokane, Washington, after a couple years he was offered a job in Portland, Oregon and then in Anchorage Alaska. He had the opportunity to interview and emcee the shows of some of the biggest names in country music. It was the 70's and the music artist we now call legends were climbing the ladder to their future hall of fame status. After our stint in Portland he had a chance to work for a station in Nashville. Before we made the decision to accept that offer and relocate he received an offer from Anchorage Alaska and since he was stationed in Alaska for one tour of duty he had always wanted to go back. Alaska was touted as the Last Frontier and held an intriguing curiosity for us. In 1974 we packed up and got ready to move to what my family called, the ends of the earth. He went first and I went to visit my family one more time. In those days it was very expensive to fly and I knew I would not be coming back for a while. I found out, the day he left for Anchorage, that I was pregnant. I joined him a couple weeks later already wearing maternity clothes. I delivered twins that fall. Although Jim said we would go to Alaska for only one maybe two years, it would end up being over 40 years. From his first night as a DJ he proved himself to be a talented announcer with the uncanny ability to name a hit song before it actually became a hit which was a benefit to the radio stations he worked for. He worked in the country music field from 1969 to 2011. During that time, he also became a real estate broker. In the earlier years of radio in Anchorage he and I had a husband and wife show that lasted for a few years. I also worked as his content director for most of his years in radio. On the radio he called me Scout, and yes there is a story to him giving me this particular endearment. My husband was not an openly romantic man however, he played and dedicated a special song to me every day that he was on the airwaves. Those songs became my I love you notes from him to me daily and for every occasion. I used to joke that his listeners could tell how much trouble he was in by the song he played for me. He was excellent at what he did, he loved his listening audience and maintained the status of being the number one country music morning show for his station's ratings until his retirement. He earned many accolades during his long radio career. Jim was chosen to be Lord Trapper for the Alaska Fur Rendezvous winter celebrations, was inducted into the Alaska Broadcasters Hall of Fame and awarded the Alaska Commendation Medal. We all lost a terrific and caring talent when he transitioned to his next adventure.

TWO

My Grief Experience

E ach death I have experienced is unique unto itself, for the sake of the length of this book, I will keep the stories short. We all know that the loss of human life is the most devastating loss of all. There is not and will never be an exact prescription for experiencing or getting through grief. We grieve over the loss of human loved ones, but we also grieve over the loss of our pets, lost loves, love gone wrong, marriages gone wrong, jobs gone wrong, careers missed, talents forgotten, the loss of who we were and time wasted. Bucket lists long yellowed and disintegrating, a life we feel we have wasted, being gone from family and friends too long, and the list can go on and on. Take a few moments to make your own list of personal losses, how many did you give yourself permission to grieve over? How many and who do you still need to get through grief over or to forgive including forgiving yourself? How much grief have you shoved deep down into your heart and soul that needs to be settled to bring peace to your heart? Should you make this list be aware that it may be quite a wakeup call. Many never equate that many losses, outside of the loss of a loved one, can fall into the realm of grief. We also learn that grief is a lifetime emotion; we never get away from grief, we only learn how to manage it. The lessons given to me early on were that grief was not to be shared or talked about. It is something one must handle by oneself. When this is the primary attitude about death, dying and grief it brings an unfortunate misunderstanding of the importance of experiencing and learning how to manage grief as it comes. I have also learned that if we do not allow ourselves to grieve in a timely manner the repercussions to our physical and mental health can take an emotional toll that can be difficult to overcome.

Birth Mother

My first lesson that grief can become a lifetime of sadness was brought on by losing my birth mother, not from death, but from absence. I was born in Missouri. My Mother and Father were divorced when I was 3, remarried, and divorced again. It was a bad divorce and my Father received custody of me, which was virtually unheard of in the 1950's. The Judge gave my Father custody on the premise that I live with my Grandmother, his mother, while my Dad served in the Air Force. While stationed in Washington State, my Dad met a woman, who would become my Step-Mother. They married and moved to Missouri to raise me and keep me within proximity to my Grandmother. I only saw my birth mother a couple of times during my Father's stint in the military. My Grandmother would put me in a cab that would take me to my birth mother's home and I would have a short visit with her. These visits were a secret, my Father could not know but my Grandmother felt it was important for me to see my Mother when the opportunity presented itself. The last time I saw my birth mother was when I was 6 years old. My Grandmother and I were walking down a street in downtown Springfield and came face to face with my mother. She kneeled to speak to me, gave me a hug and kissed me goodbye. As I watched her walk away, I had no idea that it would be the last time I would ever see or hear from her again. I remember feeling an overwhelming sadness as I watched her disappear from our view. I did not know at the time, but this would be the first-time grief gripped my heart in the form of deep sadness. Since my father would get so angry about anything that had to do with my mother, I dared not talk about her in his presence. I kept quiet about seeing my mother and prepared to meet my Stepmother. My Grandmother was my safety net, my stand-in mother, and she and I had formed a very close bond. It was very difficult for my Grandmother to see me being treated as a stepchild. It was tough on all of us that my stepmother and I could not connect with each other. When I was 8 years old, my Father moved us to Washington State to be close to her family. Intense sadness once again enveloped me as I said goodbye to my grandmother, aunts, uncles and cousins.

My Stepmothers' parents owned a farm, and that was the first place we drove to and stayed until my father could secure a job and a house for us. Their farm became my safe haven and I bonded quickly with my Stepmothers' father. He became my rock and did everything he could to help me understand why I had to toughen up being a Stepchild.

During my youth we would take vacations and drive from Washington to Missouri and spend one to two weeks visiting with my dad's and my family. This is where I truly belonged and every time we visited that intense sadness would always engulf me when we said goodbye and traveled back to Washington. I was too young to know that this intense sadness was turning into a deeper grief. The last time I saw my Grandmother was when I was 16, so the only contact I had with her after I turned 16 was through letters. I also learned that my birth mother was living in Montana and had four more children. Keep in mind that we did not have social media, so there was no way for me to secretly look her up. If I had asked my father if I could look further, the wrath of his anger would have been very unpleasant for all of us. Again, I stayed silent in my overwhelming sadness, always wondering why my mother did not contact me at all.

Paternal Grandmother

My grandmother was my first experience with losing someone so close to me to death. When she died, we couldn't afford for all of us to go to her funeral, so we sent my Father since he was her son. As time marched on, I came to understand that while I missed her, and the letters she wrote me, the feeling of grief was kept at a distance. However, I have learned since that time away from loved ones has a way of dimming the intensity of loss when it comes, and although I missed her, I had gotten accustomed to living without her in my day-to-day life. Therefore, the grief of losing her was very different than it would have been had I still lived with or near her, or saw her at the viewing and celebration of her life. I did not have to accept the reality of her being gone for a long time. Of course, I cried, and it took me a long time to not look for a letter from her. I still wrote to her-it was my therapy- but I did not mail them. I remember the day I finally threw all those letters away. Now I wish I had kept them, as they would tell my story of those years in great detail. It meant I had to fully accept that she was gone forever from us. I would now keep everything I could remember in my heart and not voice my grief. This was my second lesson of learning how to keep my grief silent.

Step Grandfather

The sudden death and loss of my Step-Grandfather held so many unanswered questions. He had become my rock and my savior within the realms of being a stepchild. He did his best to help his daughter, my Stepmother, to treat me as if I was her own. It never worked out, especially after she had 4 of her own children. He did his best to be the bridge for me in surviving a very unhappy childhood. In recent years my stepmother, now advanced in years, has said many times that I truly was the original Cinderella. I did the housekeeping, the laundry, ironing, babysat my siblings and cooked. My Father was a hard worker but fell into alcoholism and got to the point in his drinking where he was abusive and let his anger override his goodness. My Stepmother was an RN and had to work full-time to help support the family. I did not have much of a childhood nor was I a typical teenager. I had too much responsibility to partake in school and teenage activities. I left home when I turned eighteen thinking life would be better. When I was 19, my grandfather passed away suddenly. Now the full impact of losing someone who was physically in my daily life brought a different trauma than I had experienced before. The trauma of feeling completely alone with no one to go to and help me maneuver through the tough times in my life. The only safety net I felt I actually had.

Since I was not actually blood family I learned quickly that I needed to keep my grieving to myself and help everyone else get through the loss of the patriarch of my stepmothers' family. When we went to the funeral home for the viewing of my Grandfather, I had no idea what to expect. As I was standing at the side of my Grandfather's casket, my Uncle came up, took my hand and placed it on my Grandfathers hands. I stood in shock as my grandfather's hands were ice cold. I had never seen, let alone touched, a deceased person and I felt as if my feet were nailed to the floor. I could not move. Suddenly, I realized that while it looked like my Grandfather, his essence was gone. I stood, unable to move my hand. My Father came to my side and took my hand and walked me to the seating area. I was not allowed to talk to anyone about this loss or how I felt. I learned early on that grief should be handled quietly and to move on and not to talk about our loss because it upsets others.

Step Grandmother

I was not living near my family when my step-Grandmother passed away, and again, I was able to escape all the realities of death. However, I used to talk to her every week and as she got sicker she would talk to me about dying. I was the only one in the family who would allow her to talk about dying. She had a lot to say, things that she wanted others to know and I listened. This is the first time I learned that there are times when some people who know they have a small amount of time left actually wanted to talk about it. It helps to face the fears of knowing one will no longer physically exist in this world and to say everything they want their loved ones to know. I also know this is not the case of all who are aware that they are dying, so one must tread carefully, but if the one dying wants to talk about it then someone who can handle this kind of conversation needs to be called in.

I have gone through the emotions of many distant losses as Aunts, Uncles and Cousins passed away throughout the years. Again, the lessons were to keep grief to yourself.

I refer to the loss of distant relatives and friends as entering the "Misty haze of Grief".

When a family member or longtime friend who has lived apart from you for years passes away, the grief it brings is often a grief felt as in a mist. This grief is very different, and the impact of the loss seldom affects your day to day living. One still goes through many of the emotions and thoughts of, "should have, could have, wish I would have," but nothing really changes in your day to day living.

Best Friend

The day came when I had to face the loss of one of my very best friends to Multiple Sclerosis and once again, I was caught in the shadows of grieving alone and silently because it made others uncomfortable to talk about her and her illness. I cried silently and alone and would fight for composure every time I saw her husband and children. I had met my beautiful friend in high school. She married her high school sweetheart, he joined the army and was sent overseas, and I moved in with her until his return. She was the Maid of Honor for my wedding. She and her husband moved to Alaska to be near my husband and me. We raised our children together, but after my husband and I lost our twins and she was diagnosed with MS, things changed drastically for all of us. We were all trying to deal with loss, pain and the grief of everything that was happening to us. We lost touch for a while, then her husband called and said she had passed away right after her children kissed her and left for school. Not only did our hearts break, but regret was now added to death, loss, pain and grief.

Our Twin Sons

In 1976, my husband and I were devastated by the loss of our beautiful twin boys. They were 17 and a half months old when they succumbed to carbon monoxide poisoning, a freak accident that to this day is gut wrenching. This nightmare will be with me until I take my last breath. There is a hole in my heart that will never heal, and the management of the pain is an ongoing struggle. When our little Boys died it changed my husband and me in every aspect of our life, how we viewed life and everything we believed. We lost all forms and sense of innocence. We were in Shock and the shock would never leave us. Our personalities were not so carefree anymore. We had fears we had never had. We wanted to blame someone any one. The day we lost our little boys, our innocence, our faith, our reality and who we were became altered forever. We fought to hold onto each other, not to blame each other, not to openly blame the very God we worshipped. The God who gave us these precious little boys. We did not understand. The WHY WHY WHY hounded us like a constant beating drum. We had to find how to go on. The term "New Normal" came up but the word Normal would never fit us again. There is nothing Normal about losing a child!!!!

I moved about as if in a complete Bubble of Non-existence. I was denied Grieving as it was not publicly acceptable.

It was believed that one had to be stoic and private with their grief even concerning the loss of a child. My husband turned his grief inward and expected the same of me, even when he and I were alone in our home. The pain was too great and we struggled together separately. When people asked me if we had children, I had to say no in order to not make them uncomfortable by saying "Yes, we had two little boys, but they have passed away." It was tearing me apart to not be able to share stories about these little guys who were part of our family and brought us so much joy, because it would make others uncomfortable. They were walking, talking little people who brought so much happiness to us every second of every day of their little lives. Losing a child is one of the most over-whelming and horrific losses one can experience. It changes all involved and talking about children who have passed away often puts others in an awkward position of not knowing what to say. Again, I was held to the expectation of keeping silent and handling grief quietly. Needless to say, the loss of our little boys was and is a devastating grief and pain that remains to this day.

Father

Years later, I would receive the call that my father was dying. I was not with the family and could only speak to him in his last minutes by phone. Thanks to my sisters, I was able to tell him I loved him for the last time and to thank him for all he had done for me in my life. Because I lived so far away and did not physically go through seeing him take his last breath or attend the funeral, I was able to put off my grieving for a long time and full on grief did not hit me until I visited his and my stepmothers' home a few years later. Yes, I am guilty of pretending my father was just not home when I called. By the time I visited my extended family, I had to keep my grieving private so as not to upset everyone. Once again, grief was to be kept buried deep inside in order to not cause others to be uncomfortable.

Co-Worker

One weekend I received a call from my boss. He had been out getting wood with one of our staff members and the staff member dropped dead right there on the spot. It was a shock for us all. Returning to the office was difficult. None of us realized how much we truly counted on him for parts of our jobs not to mention the personal friendships we had all acquired with each other. Sure, he had gone on vacations and his hunting trips where we had to cover some of his work, but that was only for a brief time. Now we were going to have to replace a person we all liked and never thought about the "what if he was all of a sudden never here again." Someone dying and never returning to their job is very different than someone quitting their job. Often, one's workplace becomes a second home and if that is the case, losing a co-worker will take a while to adjust to the loss. The day our coworker's wife came in to clean out his office and desk was truly a tough one for us all. No one wanted to move into that office for a few months. Slowly, we were able to make changes to move forward. We finally got to the place where we could tell the stories he was involved in that brought smiles and laughter, and allowed our work life to go forth and become productive again.

THREE

The Loss of my Husband

I n December of 2013 one of my husband's golfing buddies, tragically passed away from a stroke. To say it was a shock and devastating to all of us would be an understatement. The loss took a serious toll on my husband, and I noticed that with it, he began thinking about his own mortality more seriously. Every so often my husband would say, "Something is going to get me one day, and when it does, I hope it is quick." It was a subject that neither of us wanted to talk about, however, my husband was 73 years old and even though he did not have heart problems, neither did his friend who was only in his sixties.

In May of 2014 another of my husband's best buddies had a heart attack and was in the hospital. Jim had gone to see his friend on Thursday the 14th of May and was going back to see him again with our son on Saturday the 16th. We had decided I would visit on the 15th after work. Around 1:00 pm on the 15th my husband called and said he wanted to try out a new golf swing before the weekend and was going to drive out to his favorite golf course, located in a connecting town, while I was at the hospital visiting our friends. We had plans to attend a dance recital for one of my co-workers that evening and he assured me he would be back in time for us to make the dance recital.

As I was about to leave the hospital to meet my husband, our friend's doctor came into the hospital room and told his family that he was not doing well and there was nothing else they could do for him. They were given permission to take him home to be more comfortable. The news was devastating. I stayed with my friends a little longer and left the hospital later than I had planned. I called my husband to tell him the awful news and that I was on my way home, but he did not answer his phone. I thought he might be in the shower getting ready for our date. It registered with me that it was unusual for him not to call me or send me a text to say he was on his way home, because that was our habit. I thought he might have assumed I could not get his message in the hospital due to poor cell reception. As I came down our street towards our house and saw that my husband's truck was not in the driveway, I felt instant fear, my chest tightened and my stomach felt clinched. As soon as I pulled into our driveway, I called his phone again, but there was still no answer. At this point, I was trying not to panic. He had a hands-free system in his truck and could answer his phone while driving so I knew something was very wrong. Still, I didn't want to think he was in an accident. I went into our home and started to fix my makeup and get ready for the dance recital. I was ignoring my impending panic and proceeded as if he would arrive home any minute and tell me his phone died and traffic was the worst. It was now much later than we had planned to leave, so we needed to leave as soon as he pulled into the driveway.

Then the moment came when life stood still. I heard a knock from the door reverberate through the house. I looked out my bathroom window and did not recognize the man at my door. I was not going to go to the door since I was alone, but as I peered through the curtain, it registered that the man was wearing a uniform. All I could think was 'Oh my God, please let my husband be ok.' As I put my hand on the doorknob I knew, I just knew it was about my husband and he was not going to be ok. I opened the door and the police officer asked if I was Carolyn Schrader. I wanted to scream "No! You have the wrong house, the wrong person!" Instead, I heard myself say yes, and immediately asked if this was about my husband. As the officer began opening my door, he said "Yes Mrs. Schrader, your husband has died, are you alone? Who can you call to come be with you"? There it was. The words that would be THE life changing message one dreads to receive. "Oh my God, what the hell do you mean dead, you mean hurt!" I responded. The officer said, "No, Mrs. Schrader your husband died on the golf course. A couple golfers found him and did their best but could not revive him." The room started spinning and my head felt light, my chest became even tighter, and I could barely breathe as I heard myself literally scream-ing, "No! No! No! Not now! Not yet! Oh my God no, he can't be gone." All of a sudden, I could not remember anything or anyone's number to call. All I kept saying was "No, No, No…. You have to be wrong." The officer kept saying we needed to call someone. I vaguely remember panicking, grabbing my cell phone and saying "Our son, our son, oh my God I have to call our son." Dammit, I could not remember my own son's phone number. I finally found his number and fumbled to dial it, the officer took my phone and gave the message to our son.

At that moment, Jan and Orvel, two of our best friends, pulled into our driveway. Our friend, who owned the golf course, had called them hoping they could get to me before the police did. Jan and Orvel had been our closest friends for over 30 years. Orvel and Jim were avid year around golfers. I managed to call our neighbor, Donna, and she came running over right away. She and her husband Cliff had been our friends and neighbors for almost 25 years. They are living with their own loss and grief. Their adult son, Matt, had recently passed away from a motorcycle accident. Another, all of a sudden, death that can never be healed. And still they came for me and my son and his family to help us navigate this horrific night and the weeks to come. Our son arrived, my daughter-in-law and granddaughters came shortly after. Everyone was in as much shock as I was. We had no warning, no sign of impending health issues. What the hell???? The upset, confusion, and disbelief were overwhelming. To make matters worse, one more dose of reality hit, our son was deploying in two weeks. I was fighting for as much composure as possible without much success. I kept going back and forth from shock to feeling like I had entered some portal to hell. At some point my son asked me if I needed some water and my response was "Hell no, give me a shot of whiskey." I felt like I was watching everything and everyone from a distance and in a hazy light.

I worked as a Military Family Assistant Coordinator and was required to carry a 24/7 emergency phone. I knew I was not in the frame of mind to look up resources for a military family that may need help, therefore I had to get in touch with another staff member. When we reached one of my co-workers, she thought we were saying our friend in the hospital had passed away. By the time it became clear we were talking about my husband she went into shock with the rest of us. My mind was reeling back and forth between "Oh my God" and "What the Hell." Random thoughts came and went like an out of control movie. My son, my daughter-in-law and my beautiful little granddaughters, what on earth are they to do with this, without their father, father-in-law and papa? He and I will never have what 'we' were going to have, do what 'we' were going to do, be who 'we' were going to be. Who in the hell was I supposed to be without him? Who was going to take care of us and protect us while our son is deployed protecting our freedom? My husband and I were devoted supporters of our military, therefore there was no question whether our son should or should not deploy. As hard as it was going to be on all of us, he had to go, he had a job to do and his team was counting on him. His dad would have never wanted to be the reason, even in death, for our son not to fulfill his military obligations and do what he had to do.

We only had minimal contact with my husband's daughter from his second marriage, our son called her and gave her as much information as we had at the time. It felt like time was standing still while also passing at record speed. The authorities would not allow us to go see my husband because he died in another county and they had to investigate his death and make sure it was from natural causes. I kept pleading to be taken to my husband, my God, he was laying out on that golf course without his family by his side and only strangers taking care of him. Our friends were doing their best to take care of us on all levels while dealing with their own shock and pain. They held us, talked with us, cried with us and did their best to make sense of it all, especially when the police man told me I could not go to the golf course to be with my husband. I realized I had better call our friends at the hospital and let them know my husband and son would not be there as planned. I called the daughter of our friends and when she answered I told her that I had bad news, and that my husband, her dad's best friend, had died that afternoon. She, as expected, went into shock and disbelief. My husband had come to the hospital a couple days before and looked just fine. I told her it was a shock for all of us and to please let her mother know. My friend's daughter and husband rushed over to console us and told us they had decided not to tell her father. They thought it would be too much for him in his last stages of life. I certainly understood but felt saddened that her father would pass away never knowing why my husband did not come to see him one more time. By this time, my son, his family, our neighbor and friend were just sitting in a daze with me still saying, "What the hell, what are we to do, why did I not know if something was wrong?" Our friend from the golf course reminded us that she knew nothing either when her husband died. He had gone to bed and the next thing she knew he was gone. However, my mind kept going back over the last month for a sign, any sign that I should have caught about his health.

Then the call came, my son answered the phone. "We have brought Mr. Schrader's body to Anchorage and he will be at the morgue." They said we could come and see my husband soon. The morgue, those words, "the morgue", those were the words that brought me to my knees. What did "soon" mean? I was told he died somewhere around 2 or 3 in the afternoon and it was now almost midnight, so 'soon' didn't mean much to me. Then the next call that came was right out of hell as far as I was concerned. The caller identified themselves as a living donor's company and asked if we would be willing to donate parts of my husband's body for the sake of saving others. I cannot even begin to tell you what that call did to us. We were desperately trying to handle the fact that my husband was dead and now this. I now understand that they truly are not trying to make it more difficult for us as time is of the essence and critical to the process. However, to have to make that kind of decision when we were already entrenched in deep shock was unbearable for me and our son. My son looked at me and said, "Mom this is up to you." I was as devastated as was he. I made the decision with our sons' agreement, and gave them permission to take what would help another to live. I could not contain my crying or swearing for that matter.

Somewhere close to midnight, our friends Jan, Orvel, Donna and my son and his family left. Our friend, the one who lost her husband five months prior, said she would stay the night with me. Of course, there was very little sleep to be had and when daylight hit, everything started all over with reality hitting us full on. My son had to go to the golf course to get his father's truck. Then he had to go to the police station to receive his father's phone, wallet, watch, glasses and sunglasses and whatever else my husband had in his pants pocket. When my son brought his father's belongings home, all we could do was set them on the table and stare at them for what seemed like forever. I had to go out to the trash can, forgetting that my husband's truck was now in the driveway, when I opened the garage door my heart seemed to lurch forward into my chest, panic and the harsh reality hit even harder.

The decision was made to have my husband cremated. The trip to the funeral home was the second longest trip I have ever made. The first longest trip was also to this same funeral home for the funeral of our little twin sons. The funeral home was beyond kind in their caring for us. They helped us maneuver the legalities, as my son was deploying, and we needed to have so much done before he left. My husband's brother flew in to help us. It was very comforting to have him with us. Our neighbors, friends and co-workers came and went bringing food and offering to help in any way we needed. The Chaplains from the base I worked on came to offer condolences and comfort. My beautiful and talented Co-Workers, or my Divas as I called them, provided much of the daily support I needed to get me through and in keeping me level and balanced. These ladies were more like my daughters and granddaughters and remain in touch with me to this day.

At the end of the week, we got a call from the funeral home that my husband's ashes were ready to be picked up. I cannot even begin to tell anyone what it was like and how surreal it was when the funeral director handed me the urn with my husband's ashes. As I got into the car and buckled my seat belt it struck me beyond hard that I was holding all that was left of my 6'2' husband in my lap. I could not say anything I could only cry all the way home.

We, with the help of our beloved friends, held an Irish wake for my husband. I made the decision to put his urn in his golf bag and put the bag in the living room during his wake. It was less stressful to look at his golf bag than his urn. I felt it was very fitting and knew he would have appreciated it as a fitting ending. Time was running out for us, and our son's deployment was fast approaching. My husband never wanted to leave Alaska so our son and I agreed that he would take his father's ashes, after he returned from deployment, and scatter them on a mountain that overlooked another mountain known as "The Sleeping Lady." This mountain was a legend to Alaska and had an endearing and important meaning to my husband and me. It was the first thing my husband showed me and told me about when he picked me up at the airport the day I landed in Alaska 42 years before.

Our son deployed and my daughter-in-law, granddaughters and I held on tight to each other as our friends held onto us. The next two months were fraught with hard lessons that made it clear that I had not been ready to lose my spouse. I sold my husband's truck. Our beloved and closest friends bought his truck to use in their business, and it helped me with immediate finances. I had to get all the utilities in my name. The bank where we had our accounts for the last 30 years is a membership bank and since my husband was the primary account holder, that made me a co-primary, and as such, they would not allow me to keep our account, line of credit nor would they put my home in my name only. I had to open a brand-new account, start all over for credit and I had only one year to clear all the old transactions and automatic deposits in our shared account.

I would soon learn that without a will (which my husband did not have), one would have many more difficulties than need be. I found out that most of the "in case of death", insurance we paid for on our credit cards and our home had been cancelled when my husband turned 70. By rights, my home should have been paid off at the time of his death. Not so. The bank had sent a letter to my husband informing him they were cancelling the death insurance when he turned 70. A letter I had not seen. I found one small life insurance policy that was still intact which allowed me to pay off most of our debts. A blessing I thank my husband for every day.

While going through the realities of what life will now look like for me, my mind was constantly meandering with so many thoughts. Now, I have come to realize these scattered thoughts and emotions are all part of the grief walk that is mine alone. I read many of the articles that tell us what to expect when one's spouse has passed away. I kept going over and over our lives and events that happened before that horrible knock on my door. I will forever feel sorry for that poor policeman who had to be the one to knock on my door and deliver the devastating message to me.

It is taught that there are five stages of grief one goes through. Now, they say there are seven. I will say that not only are there a few more than five or even seven stages the grief we experience greatly depends on the type of loss we are going through. Nothing about grief is as neatly packaged as the word 'stages' evokes. We must keep in mind that in 1969 when Elizabeth Kubler Ross originated the five stages of grief they were written for those who have been told they haven't much time left, not for those who remain after a loved one dies. In later years Kubler Ross and her co-author David Kessler wrote two books better clarifying the original stages of grief. (Life Lessons, Two Experts on Death & Dying Teach Us About the Mysteries of Life & Living) (On Grief & Grieving, Finding the Meaning of Grief Through the Five Stages of Loss).

FOUR

Unpredictability of Shock and Grief

W ith the death of my husband I learned again that grief is intensely personal and no one, family, friends, society or books can tell you how to grieve and how long to grieve. The lists of components and levels to grieving are as long as there are people who have reasons to grieve. The types of grief, the circumstances surrounding the grief and the reason for the grief are a thousand-fold. For over forty years I have helped others navigate through all forms of grief and, even with my years of experience and knowledge, I can tell you that when the shock of hearing the policeman tell me my husband was dead I was not subdued at all in my reaction. I did not sit down on the bench in our entryway and begin crying quietly about the news. My repeated "No, no, no" became louder as I was becoming more panicked and the shock was deepening. I am generally the person who stays calm amid a crisis. However, the state of being calm was nowhere in sight. I have learned from my past encounters with crisis that shock does more than throw you into an emotional war of feelings and thoughts. Shock can protect you, your mind, emotions, and body from going into violent responses to the crisis that has just hit with the force of a cannon. Shock can also cause one to react uncharacteristically, depending on the type of crisis you're facing. Shock depends on the support you have around you and your very own personal nature in responses to any given crisis.

When our little boys passed away, shock completely numbed me, and I seemed to move through everything like a zombie, absent of all awareness of those around me. I felt completely lifeless and did everything as if I had become a robot. When my husband died, shock threw me straight into disbelief and panic. I felt sick to my stomach and began shaking so hard I could hardly hold my phone to call my son. As the evening wore on, shock held me in exhaustion, in total disbelieve, and in a myriad of contradictions. Shock also held me in a suspended state, with time seeming to stand still while at the same time seeming to spin forward at a speed I could not catch up to.

In the loss of a loved one, the state of disbelief and remnants of shock will come and go forever. There is also an aftershock, not unlike the way earthquakes and their aftershocks are recorded. In my aftershock, I was still in a state of disbelief. It was hard to get my head around the fact that my husband was absolutely gone. He was not going to come walking through the door, down the hallway or open the garage door asking for help or for me to come see his latest golf swing. I would begin to fix dinner then stop, saying to myself, "What are you doing, you are only one now, remember?" I kept my husband's favorite ice-cream in the freezer for a year after he passed away. I just couldn't bring myself to throw it away even though I was not going to eat it. I found it was in these little things that caused me the most difficulties in letting go, so many habits that came from 46 years of being married to the same person.

Grieving is about experiencing loss. It is about letting go of the way we thought life was going to be. It is being ok with feeling sorry for ourselves for a little while, because an event happened in our life that we not only did not want, but also that we did not have any control over. It is about realizing we have no control of anything. As far as time goes, we only have this very moment we are in. It is about dealing with the realization that life is fragile and limited. There is an ending and none of us know when that ending will march in and say, 'this is it, come with me.' Grieving is about releasing the inner pressure of panic, pain, shock, the unknown and crying it all out until you cannot cry anymore, at least for the moment. I knew that if I did not allow myself to go through my grief, this time, to cry when I needed to cry, to yell and scream if I needed to, to cuss and rant and rave about the unfairness and get it out and off my chest, it would be very damaging to my emotional and physical health at this point of my life. It was time to deal with all of the grief I was not allowed to grieve openly about throughout my life.

Wee Hours of the Morning.

Some of the loneliest times will be in the wee hours of the mornings. The Always, Nevers, Should Haves, Could Haves and the Little Things I would think about in the wee hours of the morning would bring me into disbelief all over again. Every time I laid down my thoughts would begin racing in rampant patterns, running from the first time I met my husband to the life changing knock at the door. It seemed like I was reliving every year of our life from the day we met.

Making myself lay down in the hopes of getting some sleep, any amount of sleep, became a nightly battle. I would often have to get up and walk off my panic about life without my husband, fear of my own death and any other fear that befell me. Many times, I would turn up my music until I could change the trajectory of my thoughts. I had friends, dear friends who said "Call me if it gets too much," but calling someone at 2 or 3 a.m. would soon become too much for them. I had to find my own way of controlling my thoughts in hopes of getting even two hours sleep, or more if at all possible. This was most difficult while working a full-time job. I slept in my recliner instead of going to bed. The bed was too big with him gone and way too damn empty.

I have thought many times about how little we really know about the complete role our spouses play in our lives and in taking care of all the things that need to be done concerning the up keep of our homes. Many of the things they do seem to slide into "the little things" box and just get done. Some were simple tasks, some more difficult, some tasks my husband did were done without me knowing they needed to be done and some totally out of my knowledge and skill level. The simple things I can, of course, do but the more difficult tasks I will have to hire someone to help with.

Sometimes, it was the little things that really threw me. My husband always climbed the ladder while I held it to change our hall, garage and outdoor light bulbs. I am not steady enough to climb that ladder and if I did, I would have to have a friend or neighbor come over to just hold the ladder or have our son run over to change the lights that were too high to reach without a ladder. My husband always picked up the dead mouse in our garage. I never gave it a second thought when I would go running to him while screeching about a mouse in the garage again. He would laugh at me, shake his head and dispose of the "big scary creature".

He always went around the house changing all the clocks on daylight saving time and would double check my phone to be sure it also changed. He took care of the yard and I planted the flowers. I took primary care of the inside of our home, getting the groceries and taking care of him. His part was to fix things, take care of our cars and yard. My husband took care of our vehicles, making sure the oil was changed, made sure we had fluid for our windshield wipers, got our tires changed when needed, and even made sure my car stayed washed and clean. Whether we would have a catastrophic leak or little leak from a pipe inside or outside the house, my husband was the one who climbed down into the crawl space to turn the water off and fix the leak. Hell, I didn't even know where the water valve was and there was no way I would go into that crawl space anyway! Now, not only did I have to worry about anything leaking, but I had to worry about climbing down that crawl space and trying to find that damn valve to turn off the water. So many things I realized that were now my responsibility, things I really never gave a thought to because he just took care of them.

It was difficult for me to stay focused on the emotional task of going through my husband's things and his golf equipment in the garage. One day, as I stood in the middle of the garage looking at his tools, golf equipment, and garage stuff I just felt so overwhelmed that I decided an easier task was to wash my car. I filled a bucket with soapy water and went out to get the hose to wet down my car. My husband loved new gadgets and had a new gadget on the hose. Of course, I could not figure out how to work this new gadget. I tried everything, and yet no water. For crying out loud, it is just a damn hose, what the hell? I kept wrangling with the end of the hose until I couldn't take it anymore. In frustration, I threw the hose across the yard and started crying right there in the middle of my driveway. This would become one of many frustrated outbursts I would have. Damn it! We had it all worked out, he had his "things" he just "always" did, and I had mine, and it all worked well. We were from that 'era' where the man had his duties and the woman had hers. So many things I cannot even begin to list, yet I found consistently that most of the biggest frustrations came from "the little things."

He was not perfect, I am not perfect, and we were not perfect. By today's standards in relationships, we were really old fashioned. But it worked for us.

At times, the negative memories of life will creep into our thought processes about our loved one. This is not to remind us that there was pain within our relationship, but because we have come to resent time spent on anything that was not wonderful and happy with our loved one. This relates to all losses from grandparents to spouses. Thoughts of guilt like "I should have, I could have, and I wish I would have" will arise out of the mists of grief. Often two of the hardest to deal with is; "I wish I had" and "Why didn't I" which seems to always follow a loss.

We will think back at some of our tough times and realize how differently we could have handled them.

Crying is not only important but often a necessity

Crying is a release of pain, sadness, a heart full of emotions, frustrations, happiness, confusion and loneliness. There are many studies about the importance of crying. According to Joseph Stromberg of the Smithsonian's Collage of Arts and Science, tears contain organic substances and have distinct molecules. Tears take on different shapes and forms depending on the reason for the tears. His studies show that tears brought on by peeling an onion, tears of change, tears of grief, tears of happiness and so on look very different from each other. However, be aware that not crying while grieving should not cause alarm and not crying in no way means the grieving is any less.

I have learned that others become uncomfortable when tears are shed over losses. Most people don't know what to do or say, so they will back off or avoid any conversation about another person's loss. I was told to be strong, to not think about it, to get a handle on my emotions, and to seek professional help, when in fact I was simply releasing my pain, sadness and the pressures grief brings. Grief and tears that are a result of grief will come anytime and anywhere. It has been years since my little boys passed away. There are times when I am asked about them and I can tell their story and get through it without breaking down, and there are times when I will barely get started talking about them and fall completely apart again. Memories will bring unpredictable and unexpected emotions at any given time.

Just the other day my family and I went to a vegetable farm for a Halloween corn maze and pumpkin patch event, and as I sat down on a bench in the shade waiting for my granddaughters to pick out their pumpkins, I looked up and right in front of me was a John Deere tractor with a hay wagon attached. Memories of my Grandfather came flooding back as if I were back on the farm with him again. Trust me when I say that memories from our losses will come at any time and many times, they will bring tears.

I have been asked what the rule of thumb should be for when one needs to get professional help in working through their grief. First of all, there is not a "rule of thumb" when someone needs professional help. However, there are some signs to watch out for. When a person in grief absolutely has no one to talk to about their loss and is unable to talk out their grief. When they enter depression and cannot seem to pull out of it. When they stay in bed more than they get up and get busy. When they are nonstop crying and becoming so exhausted that they are unable to do anything. When they are isolating themselves from family and friends. When their pain outweighs their ability to respond in any other way than crying. There is no shame in seeking help to get through or handle grief. Grief is a very complicated emotion for everyone and everyone suffers grief very differently. Even if someone has the same type of loss it is not the same in grief. There may be similarities, but it is never, never the same. I finally gave myself permission to shed my tears when they came. To cry when I needed to even if I had to go to my car to do so. I fought back and held my tears for so long through so much grief that they seemed to be hitting me in waves from one memory to another. Allow yourself to cry, it is healthy, it is tension releasing, it is healing!

It is ok to sit with your grief, to cry it out, to be angry, to be in disbelief, to give respect and the time your grief needs. Crying allows you to release the tension of grief and gives one the ability to think clearly and introspectively about life as it will now become. It is important to have family members and friends who will sit with a person who is grieving, allowing the griever to cry and will even cry with them. Even as a grief coach, I have shed a few tears while with a grieving family member, friend and client. It is all part of getting through and helping another get through. Grief never leaves us, we can only learn to manage our thoughts and our emotions that bring sadness and pain to us. There is a loss involved in every ending and will always bring lessons about ourselves while going through it. With every loss we are changed in some way.

Laughing is good even in grief

Let me say once and for all that it is ok to laugh. It does not make anyone insensitive to the loss. In fact, there will be moments that a memory will bring up uncontrollable laughter about something said or something done by the one we have lost.

I remember an incident at my husband's celebration of life that caused many of the guests to react a bit negatively. Our son's teammates, the ones he was deploying with, came to support our son in the loss of his father. Our son had set up a gathering place in the garage with the door open for ease of extra space. One of the team members was tasked with bringing a flower arrangement for the family. It was one of the most beautiful porcelain vases, in the shape of a pitcher, I had ever seen, and it was filled with dozens of flowers. He opened the door from the garage to the kitchen, one hand holding this very heavy vase filled with water and flowers, the other holding the door. As he stepped into the kitchen the hand holding the vase started shaking with the weight of the vase. He was desperately trying to get it to the kitchen counter to set it down, all the while spilling water everywhere. My daughter-in-law saw what was happening and tried to get to him to help.

At that moment, the garage door opened and my son started to walk in. When he saw his teammate in a panicked but comical situation, the look on my son's face alone caused us to start laughing, then we started laughing even harder when my son quickly stepped back into the garage instead of helping to save his buddy. By this time, which was only in seconds and minutes, I was also running to reach the young man to help set the vase down. By the time we all got to him he had finally reached the counter. Seeing that all eyes were now on him, this poor young man was so embarrassed and mortified he didn't know what to say. I thanked him and told him it was ok, that the vase and flowers were beautiful, and we would take it from there. As my daughter-in-law and I started mopping up the water, while trying not to go in and out of hysterical laughter, he bolted out to the garage to join his buddies.

We loved the magnificent arrangement, but it was the several minutes of laughter that broke the somberness of the gathering. I found a few guests looking aghast at the fact that my family and I were all laughing. Heaven forbid I or anyone should laugh at anything other than a memory brought up, or of a humorous story, or something the deceased had said or done. When in a grieving situation, especially during a celebration of life, there will be many different attitudes present about what grieving should look like. There will be some who believe that grieving should be constant crying and sadness, at least for a year or so. The fact is, emotions come and go so fast within the grieving process that you can find yourself lurching from hysterical laughing right into hysterical crying. It happens, and it is ok! Laughing is as healing as crying is. There will be times we laugh over the silliest of things out of sheer exhaustion and not only won't be able to stop ourselves, but we will go right into crying until we have no emotion left at that moment.

FIVE

Regrouping

M y husband passed away in early May, our son deployed the end of May and in July, my daughter-in-law made reservations to travel to several dance competitions for my granddaughters. We were still in shock and needed to change things up, get away and regroup. I had made the decision to retire by the end of the year, however, my company was in the process of making some major changes and it would be better for both the company and me if I retired at the end of July instead. I needed this trip, my family needed this trip, but most importantly, we needed to get away to give our hearts a break from the constant reminders of what was now no more. I was fortunate enough to have an extremely qualified co-worker to turn everything over to and the work we did would not miss a beat.

We traveled from Alaska to Seattle to California to Washington, D.C. then to Arizona. The competitions kept our minds busy; we were still in shock and total disbelief that my husband was gone and the heaviness of concern over the deployment my son was on. Our son had deployed so many times that we all had found our own way to handle our fears until his return. He was Special Forces, and as such he and his team were highly trained and focused for the job they had to do. They were trained how to stay focused no matter what was going on personally. He always had a way to get into his own mental preparedness for going into war, but no matter how focused his training was, this time he would be fighting a war with a heavier heart. I would not allow myself to think of the dangers my son was facing nor would I allow myself to think of returning to an empty home. I refused to feel guilty for taking this trip, or as some viewed it, this vacation. I needed to give myself mental, emotional, physical and heart space to try to regroup my thinking. Right after we arrived in Seattle, my mother, two of my sisters, and two of my nieces joined us for two days. They were in their own state of disbelief over the death of my husband and the deployment of my son. It helped to see extended family and talk about my husband and what he had accomplished in his life. In California, we visited my daughter-in-law's family. It was really good for my granddaughters to visit with their grandparents, aunt, uncle and cousins. It also gave my daughter-in-law a chance to just be for a while and to have her parents, sister, brother, aunts and cousins take up space in her heart and thoughts.

My daughter-in-law was very close to my husband. He absolutely adored her, after all, she and our son gave us two of the most joyful gifts ever, our granddaughters. Every time our son deployed, my daughter-in-law knew she and the girls could count on my husband to help and fix anything that broke. Our granddaughters were Papa's girls from their first breath.

In Arizona we visited my husband's younger sister whom he hadn't seen in a few years. We showed her the last photos taken of her brother and it warmed our hearts when she said he looked so happy. We held it together throughout our trip even when we were with family. It helped to be completely out of our norm and away from the harsh reality we were now living in. They all marveled at how strong we all seemed to be, and I marveled at how we pulled off this observation. 'Strong' is a word that one hears way too often when in the middle of trying to maneuver through grief or any crisis for that matter. It seems like every other person is telling us to "Be strong," or, "You are so strong, you can handle this," or, "You must be strong for those around you." I can say that for me, the word 'strong' at a time of struggle, pain and intense grief becomes an offensive word. I don't "need to" or "must be" anything when I am trying to get through the depths of a hell I did not ask for.

Our new, harsh reality came back with a vengeance as we were on the plane heading for home. My daughter-in-law said that she and the girls were going to stay with me until school started, as she thought it would help us all. What we were not sure of was that staying together at my home would be ok for the girls. We landed, gathered our bags and took deep breaths knowing that driving into my driveway would bring it all back. Walking into the house we felt the difference. The house was different. The air was different. It felt like a house, not a home. My husband's bathrobe still hung behind our bedroom door. His clothes and shoes were still in our closet. Everything about him was still there, except him. The emptiness in our hearts that we had managed to keep at bay came crashing down on all of us. We just sat and cried. It is amazing how busy we can get in order to not take on our realities or allow the thoughts, that are waiting to hit like a sledge hammer, to come thundering down. We knew these thoughts and realities were just waiting to come barreling down and buckle us at the knees. We were relieved to see that the girls found comfort being around their Papa's stuff.

When school started, my daughter-in-law and granddaughters went back to their home. As they drove away, I slowly closed the door and there it was! There would be no stopping that all-encompassing silence. Nothing can be more deafening than silence after a loss. It was time to completely deal with my loss, my grief, my pain and my anger. Yes, anger. In 1976 my husband and I lost little twin boys at seventeen and a half months old from carbon monoxide poisoning. I remembered that a few months after my little boys passed away, I found myself standing in my dining room crying and once again screaming "WHY." All of a sudden, I had felt as though I could pick up my formal oak dining room table and hurl it through our plate glass window without any effort at all. I knew the anger of grief, the anger of the word "WHY" and the intense negative power that anger can bring to us.

I knew I needed to just sit down and pull myself together and get my anger under control. Trashing my home may feel good in the moment, but it was not the long-term answer to my anger. I grabbed a bottle of wine, yes, I said bottle, and sat in my "moment chair" and proceeded to cry, cuss, be angry, be sad, be sorry, and be alone. My moment chair was a chair that sat in front of our large picture window and looked out over a beautiful treed greenbelt. I always sat in this chair when I needed to give serious thought to anything that came up and needed to make a tough decision. This was my go to place of contemplation if I was upset and needed to think about issues that were causing me or us problems or if I just needed to be creative.

After a while I began laughing, because I knew that if my husband could see me at this time, he would be absolutely perplexed at my all-consuming pity party. I was ok with that thought and I partied on!

He had said that if he went first, he wanted me to get on with my life immediately. As I took another drink of my wine, I said to him (yes, I still talked to and at him), "Right, I'll just do that, not! Are you 'flipping' kidding me, you did leave first and there is no 'immediately' going to happen about anything. I can't believe you actually left me, your family and your damn golf clubs."

Yep, I said that, and I am not sorry. It is how I felt at that moment of intense pain and fear. There will be many things we may say, or at least think, that would probably shock those who have never experienced the anger that a death can bring. Know that it is ok to vent, and it's ok to be angry. To cry, to cuss, to ask why, to feel all alone, to feel fear, allow your pain, experience all that is needed to release the emotions that are storming within you. Just don't just unpack and stay there! We must move through each level as best we can. One of the harshest lessons I learned when we lost our little sons was that the question of "Why" will NEVER be answered! While you may be asking yourself that big 'why,' know that it is a question that will take you into a mental imprisonment that is difficult to come out of. Ask, then move on! Learn to sit in silence, prayer or meditation so you can hear what ever answers may come.

I finally came to the place I had been avoiding. It was time to start simplifying the contents of the house my husband and I had lived in for 25 years. To say the least, this was an extremely daunting task. My son was still deployed, and my daughter-in-law and grand-daughters would be busy with school. I find it somewhat ironic that I had spent a big part of my work life being a grief counselor, yet now, once again I would learn even more about myself and how to once again walk my own path of pain and adjustment to a major loss and life change. I have lost grandparents, aunts, uncles, cousins, friends, two children and now my spouse. I can tell you that every loss comes with its own grief process. With every loss comes lessons we did not even know we needed, and with every loss we change. We are not only no longer the person we were, we definitely will not become the person we were going to become.

When I finally laid down to sleep, that first night of being completely alone, it was a struggle to keep my eyes closed and a struggle to keep the rampaging thoughts under control. Somewhere in the wee hours of the morning (and we already know how dangerous those can be,) I fell asleep, only to awake with the thundering silence of reality; this was really it, and my life as I knew it was over. I was at the page of our storybook that read "The End."

For forty-six years I had carved out an identity for myself as 'Jim's wife.' Who the hell am I going to be now? I was no longer a wife, I was no longer part of a couple and I was no longer employed. I searched my heart and soul to find something to be grateful for in that moment of self-crisis. One of the best coping mechanisms I found after my grandfather passed away was to think of and talk about all of the things I was grateful for that he had taught me. As I would talk about our fun times on the farm I realized that my sadness lightened. When I found myself heading into the immense and devastating emotions of losing our little boys I fought my way back by talking about all the happiness, love and laughter they brought to us. I have learned over and over that the practice of being grateful about the simplest things along with the big things in my life can bring me back to a breathable place in my heart, soul and overall well-being. I have been starting and ending my days with at least three things I am grateful for everyday for years now.

The first things that came to me that first night was how grateful and thankful I was to have had my husband with me for all those years, to still be a mother and a grandmother. I was thankful for the friends that stayed close to help me through this nightmare. Feeling restless, I got up made myself a cup of coffee and sat in my "moment chair."

I sat there, looking at the lawn, and registering that it needed mowing. That's when another reality hit me square on. I realized how little I knew of what needed to be done to winterize my home. Good grief, another thing my husband had just taken care of, especially since he had retired. I needed to check my husband's office in hopes I could find a list of things to be done to prepare for winter. My husband had a habit of making lists of things to get done, something we started when we owned our motor home. I searched his desk and sure enough there it was, the winterize home list. Yay! A win for once. I also had begun my own list of the things I needed to do so I wouldn't forget anything now that I had my chores and his to do.

I stayed busy, at night I kept lights on throughout the house, as well as music and tv. I was still only able to sleep in two-hour increments. This house was very different with just me in it. I had only been alone a handful of times in the forty-six years we had been married, but all of a sudden, after living in this house for 25 of those years, I realized it had many sounds I had never heard before. I did not have a dog or an alarm system, my husband was always here to be my knight in shining armor in the night when something did not sound right. I finally dosed off in my chair and when morning came, I started the process of removing his clothes, coats and shoes.

Everyone must address this in their own time. The sad realities are that the end of our life so much of the stuff we accumulate will either end up sold, gifted, donated or taken to the dump. Very little is wanted by our adult children or grandchildren.

I went through all of my husband's clothes. I kept telling myself this was no different than when he and I would purge our clothes and get rid of the ones we did not want. Then I would come to one of his favorite shirts and start crying all over again. I even put one on that I particularly loved him in while finishing this sad task. I separated the shirts that were his favorites and the ones that he wore often and set those aside. For those, I asked my family if any brought specific memories to them, and if so, did they want me to make something from them, like a pillow, or quilt or if they just wanted them. My Granddaughters picked a couple button up shirts from the stack and wore them as night shirts, and I will admit I also chose a couple to wear as night shirts and shirt jackets. I felt better giving his good clothes to those who could use them. We always did this when we cleaned out our closets. One of the articles of clothing I put aside was his work jeans with paint and glue dried on them, again it was a sentimental save for the time being.

I gave our neighbor Cliff, who was about the same size as my husband, a jacket that had a country music logo on it from the radio station my husband worked for. I donated my husband's motorcycle leathers and helmet to a Vets motorcycle group he highly supported. Then I called an agency to come pick up the rest of the many bags I had filled. I put them out on my front walkway and closed the door.

I would get up numerous times, and open the door with the intention of bringing all the bags back in. Each time I would close the door and tell myself no, this had to be done, leave them alone. After a few trips I finally decided that no, I was not ready. I went to the door, opened it, and they were gone. I don't know how long I just stood at the door looking at the empty walkway crying. In the next months I slowly began to go through everything else. I took photos of everything I wanted to archive and filed them in my husband's memory folder on my external hard drive to be safe.

Removing Books and hobbies

I took all my Husband's books and sorted those that were collectables. He had some his father passed down to him that were in leather and autographed by the authors, and for those I asked my family and friends if there were any of those left that they wanted to read. What no one else wanted I took to our community library, veteran centers and senior centers.

Removing Pictures

My husband had many paintings and framed pictures of B52 Bombers, Bi-Planes and other aircrafts. I asked family and friends if anyone wanted them. The ones that they did not want, I donated for auction at our local aviation museum. Yes, I could have sold them, however, it just made me feel better to support an organization my husband always supported and took our out of town guest to see, telling them all about the history of Alaskan aviation.

Removing tools and Garage stuff and things

Going through our garage was a similar process. After I put aside items that were specific to me, and a few things I knew I would need to continue to take care of my home, I asked my son to look at the rest. Most of the golf stuff we donated to a young man who taught children and young teens to golf. I sold the few clubs and bags that only fit someone my husband's size. My son took almost all his Dad's tools and tool chest, of which my husband had intended for him. Everything else would either be sold, donated or taken to the dump. It may seem harsh, but that is reality.

Everything he ever wore was gone, except his bathrobe, which still hung on the back of our bedroom door and a couple keepsake shirts. I went to our bedroom, put his bathrobe on and crawled into bed on his side of the bed. I stayed there for a while, processing another ending, another reality and another emotional change. When I got up, I hung his bathrobe back on the hook behind our bedroom door where it belonged and where it would stay, at least for now.

Important Note

Please make sure that any time a loved one's items such as; clothing, books, games, keepsakes and so on that are being removed it is done at the discretion of the surviving spouse and not by a well-meaning relative or friend. No one knows what is important to keep more than the remaining spouse, parents or the next in line to the deceased. When our little boys passed away my husband and friends came in and cleared out their bedroom. They boxed up all their clothes and toys then took apart their cribs and took them away. They all, including my husband, thought they were doing the right thing and that by removing everything would help me get through this horrible time. I say to everyone DO NOT DO THIS!! My husband told me that they packed the baby's things in boxes and a friend was going to store them until I could go through them. Sadly, I was never able to find those boxes with their clothes, toys and the professional photos we had of them. No one could remember where they went. I highly caution everyone that if anyone is boxing up a deceased loved one's belongings that they put the boxes where the spouse, parents or family can find them when they are ready to go through them. This is a heartbreak I will never get past. It was devastating to have others take away physical memories of my babies.

After going through this heavy-hearted distribution of my

husband's belongings my neighbor came to my rescue and helped me get almost everything done for winterizing my home. We mowed the lawn one more time, washed down the deck, pulled all the dying flowers up and took down the hanging flower baskets. We washed and cleaned the lawn mower and put into the shed, washed the windows, driveway and walkway then unhooked the hoses and drained them and put into the shed as well. Yes, I knew all this needed to be done, but I was still in enough shock that I needed help organizing myself to get it all done. My neighbor was my stabilizer. Fortunately, my son returned from deployment right before the snow hit. He took care of clearing the snow off my driveway the rest of our first winter without my husband.

As my family and I were going through our grief and doing our best to simplify, we also realized that now we were facing the "Firsts." The first year after a loved one has passed away has been referred to as the "Year of Firsts" we were told it would come at us with the furry of one bad dream after another. Our first "First" was the 4th of July, then birthdays, holidays, and back to our wedding anniversary right into the one-year mark of my husband's death. Time was moving at record and breakneck speed.

In hindsight, one of the most important life decisions my husband, our family and I made, and one I am truly grateful for, was to celebrate as much as we could before our son had to start getting ready for his deployment. On May 4th it was our youngest granddaughters' birthday, May 8th was my husband's and my 44th Wedding Anniversary, May 11th was Mother's Day, June brought Father's Day, then my husbands and my birthday in July. Our son was to deploy in three to four weeks and wouldn't return until fall, so we decided to celebrate all those milestones in one day. We celebrated our granddaughter's birthday on the 4th, then our anniversary on the 8th. On Mother's Day our son, daughter-in-law, granddaughters, my husband and I celebrated Mother's Day on the morning of the 11th, then celebrated Father's Day in the afternoon and my husbands and my birthday in the evening. We thought this was a fun way to be sure we were all together for the respective celebrations. We, of course, had no way of knowing this fun collaboration would become so profound. On May 15th my husband passed away. We were so blessed that we celebrated so much together and had such a fun time doing so before that fateful day hit us. We covered four celebrations in one day and thank God we did.

SIX

Learned Lessons Being a Widow

T he changes I had to make started immediately. As of the writing of this book I will be at or close to the five-year mark of being a widow. Right from the very start I was asking myself, "Who the hell am I supposed to be now?" I knew I had to make changes about how I thought my life should go, what I want now and who I think I want to become. The beginning of making major changes to myself, for myself and my life in general began within the week I left for our trip to the dance competitions. More dramatic changes seem to come in waves. For the first year and a half, major changes occurred monthly. It seemed that I had to make personal and financial changes every time I turned around.

I had to have some serious heart to heart talks with myself all through this life adjustment time period. I found that I felt very different when the one-year mark hit and even more different when the 18-month mark hit. The two and three-year marks brought even more prominent changes to my life as to who I was becoming, living and who was in my immediate life.

I was a completely different person at each and every mark I reached. I sat down one evening about a year after my husband passed away and made a list of things my husband and I were always going to do. Things we were going to do together, and things we were going to do separately. Then I made a list of everything I had been wanting to do if only I had more time. I then put the lists on the kitchen table to add to as thoughts came to me. After about a month I sat down with my lists and split them into two categories. The first was what I really wanted to do, and the second was the items I have had in my head for so long that I thought I really wanted to do and now not so sure. Amazingly, there were many in the second category that I found I no longer wanted to do. I especially did not want to do them without my husband. I made a new list of what I thought I wanted now. The new list was very short. I was still in a state of limbo, in shock and as I sat looking at the new list I felt like I did not really want to do a damn thing anymore, knowing full well that this was not the way to recover.

I will be the first to say crying can come at the drop of memory. A voice out of nowhere can catch me off guard, a song will come on while I am in the middle of traffic, I will pass someone who has an aftershave, shirt, or hat that takes me back, not to even mention my own thoughts and dreams. I could be going about my day doing my best to continue to hold myself together and a song comes on in the background that was a favorite of mine and my husbands and wham, the tears start. I can be at home, in my car, office, grocery store or gym and it's like getting hit by a Mac truck. Two months after my husband passed away, I was driving to work and a commercial that my husband had recorded for the radio station he worked for came on. Suddenly, there was his voice telling everyone to go to a particular establishment. I had to pull over to gather myself.

Tears will well up at some of the most inopportune times. One day I walked into a clothing store and they had just put out some men's shirts and I walked right over thinking my husband would love these and the new summer colors before the hit came that he was no longer here. It took me a few months to quit buying my husband's favorite candy. So many things that had become habit or automatic for so many years did not end when losing a spouse. You must completely retrain yourself and set different ways of doing things to break those habits.

More to think about.

Selling, giving away or throwing away any of your deceased spouse's belongings is a strictly personal timeline for the one grieving to decide. Don't do any of this until it feels right, or until it has been done for the sake of the griever, financial reasons or the timing is imperative. If family or friends are involved in this process, it is important to do it in the time that is best for the one grieving and their emotions.

Redoing a personal will should be an immediate priority to protect one's estate and financial holdings.

Find out what the banking and utility company's policies are concerning the death of a spouse, especially if the paperwork shows it as a joint account, before telling them your spouse has passed away. Be prepared to submit your spouse's death certificate. Do not pay off or sell a home right away until advice is sought from a financial advisor, family accountant or lawyer. Do not pay off credit cards until you know if there is a protection pay off plan in the case of the death of the main card holder. Do not tell your bank until you secure your funds are protected. My bank would not allow me to keep the account my husband and I had for over 30 years… because he was primary signer, which means he signed the first line of the signature block and I signed on the second line in the signature block. They also locked up our business account even though I made deposits into that account for business I conducted. I not only had to open a brand-new account as a new customer, but I also lost the line of credit we had built up for all those years because as a "new" customer there was no history shown. Therefore, everything I thought I had also built financially was now gone.

Making big decisions like selling a home is often emotionally tough and if it isn't financially driven then it is best to wait for a minimum of one year- even better if one can wait 18 months to two years. Two years almost to the day of my husband's passing I sold our home that we shared for 25 years of our 46-year marriage. It was to be the last home we would buy and live in until we both left this earthly life. However, keeping our home would become more of a financial burden than I was willing to deal with. I began getting the house ready to sell in January of 2016. I listed our beloved home in March and it sold and closed the first of May, which told me it was the right decision and I was doing the right thing financially. It was almost two years to the day after my husband passed away and all I asked of the real estate agent was please, do not have the closing on the date of my husband's passing. Because it was a financial necessity, it pretty much dictated the emotional decision of whether to let go or hang on. As I walked through my home the day of the closing I tried to picture the best memories from each room. As I walked out of the garage and closed it for the last time, I knew that as much as I loved this house, it would be the memories we made in this house that I would miss the most.

My thinking processes was very different after one year and even more so after 18 months. Shock had somewhat waned and I could think a lot more clearly at this time. Things looked very different to me having given myself time to figure out what the hell I was going to do with my life and "stuff and things".

There will be times when you truly need to be alone. Alone with your grief, memories, tears, and just be with yourself and your thoughts.

Know that you will mess up and that it will be lessons learned. I cannot say enough about pausing and thinking through the "what ifs", "why and why nots" before making decisions. Know it is ok to take one's time to make decisions. Unless it is another life or death scenario, most changes and decisions can wait a bit. Try to sleep on any major decisions, talk to a few others and get different thoughts on major decision-making plans.

Reading, researching and asking others who have lost spouses how they are handling things is ok, just know that each person is very different and the way they may handle and all that goes with it, is very different. We especially do not want to compare the depth nor the intensity of our grief with another's. With grief, we must take the journey of getting through in such a way that we are able to find our own management system that will get us through.

When we determine that it is now time to move forward with our different lives, we also realize that the grief of losing a spouse will always be with us. We will learn how to manage the pain and loss as time goes by, but we will always grieve for the one who is gone, the life we had and what might have been.

There will be a few friends who will abandon us. The fact is, as a widow, I have become a single female, and therefore I will not be invited to the same events I attended with my spouse. It became very obvious that if I was invited it was with the hope that I would not attend. It is unpleasant and it hurts, however, it has become my new reality. I am not offended, because I knew that if I attended an event, especially within the first year of my husband's passing, everyone would immediately feel the need to offer sympathy. I didn't want people asking how I was and how I was getting through without my husband as it would dampen the festivities the event was about. I get it now and I got it then and I was ok declining invitations that called for couples to attend.

Another realization that hit me was that I now had the time to hang out with my friends, however, they still had a spouse and could not just drop everything and hang out with me. This was another "oh yeah" moment every time I thought about calling someone to meet up with. Even if they invited me to a family gathering, I would decline, because I knew it would become about, "Poor me, lonely me, alone me," and take away from the purpose of their celebration.

I had to also learn this the hard way. I did accept a few invitations soon after my husband passed away and the moment I would walk in I could see their, "I feel so sorry for you" looks and immediately knew this was not the atmosphere I could allow myself to continue to be in. I needed friendship, support and understanding, not sympathy, sadness and pity. My best friend was great at giving me support, she texts me every morning telling me to keep going for the gusto of life and still does. I sadly realized that it may be time to let go of some of our friends. The friends who preferred that I be part of the group as a couple and I may very well never be part of a couple again. Now this could change if I have a single friend to attend with, attending with a girlfriend or a man friend, anyone that would help keep the air clear of sadness.

One of the harshest realities I had to face was accepting that I am now a single woman. Yep… single. I was very cautious of having any of my friends' husbands come to my home to help me with fixing something and always insisted that my friend also come along. Yes, I had read all of the warnings of being aware and careful of asking your friends husbands to almost become your stand in husband and come to your aid when you needed help. Therefore, I remained very cognizant of this and avoided it at all costs.

SEVEN

What People Say

One of the toughest things is not knowing what to say to someone who is in a state of shock, loss and grief. I have decided it is important to list just a few of the things said to me and I have heard said to others. I am sure everyone who is reading this can add many more to this list.

Just about everyone I have talked with, including Chaplains, say that when they meet a person in grief or someone who has just lost a loved one, they don't know what to say, so they will say the general clichés, what they think is best to say or what they have heard others say. No offense meant to anyone who has said any one of these, we all do the best we can in sad situations. I do hope this will help change how we respond to those who are experiencing loss in their life.

- The worst thing to say is "I know how you feel" or "I went through a divorce, and it was devastating." (A divorce is nothing like a person dying!)
- My friend just lost her spouse, you should get together to help each other.

- When my Mother/Father died I went through a horrible time, I know how you feel.
- I lost a child too and I know just how you feel, it is a horrible thing, I am still having trouble.
- I am sorry for your loss, if there is anything I can do, just call me.
- Oh, my how did he/she die?
- That is horrible, how are you coping?
- I am sure you will meet someone and not be alone anymore.
- Are you staying busy?
- The nights must be horrendous and lonely.
- You must be strong for your family.
- You must keep it together and not fall apart in public.
- A female friend may say "I am sure my husband knows some widowers/divorced men" he can introduce you to.
- A friend's wife will say she knows a widow or divorced friend they could introduce you to.
- We are having a few friends over on Saturday and there will be a couple single men/women there you could talk with.
- Once you lose the extra weight you have gained since your husband passed away you will find a man straight away.
- Find a younger man/woman this time.
- It must be hard and lonely to go to bed all by yourself (how do you know we did not have separate rooms, I have friends that sleep in separate rooms due to the other's snoring.)
- It has been a while now, or it's been a year now, you should be over it by now. (We never get over a death or the grief from it. We get through it and learn how to manage the pain)
- You shouldn't be crying over this after all this time.

I had a minister's wife come up to me and say, "Oh I am so sorry for your loss, you must be so lonely," I thought, well damn, thank you for that!

It will be unbelievable what others will say to you, but keep in mind they really do not know what to say and will say what they have heard others say or what they think is helping and showing that they are being sympathetic.

Always keep in mind that nobody's experience with loss will be the same or there may be similarities in their experiences but the differences can be vast. One thing many do not want to admit after losing a spouse is that perhaps their marriage was not a good one or there were many ups and downs throughout the relationship. In this case their grieving will be very different than someone whose marriage was an example of total love and devotion. Some will be totally devastated and some, although they did not wish their spouse dead, will feel a sense of relief to be out of their marriage and are fighting to not be judged for a lack of showing devastation. If negative issues plagued the relationship such as; infidelity, abuse or emotional coldness, and were not dealt with but instead pushed aside in order to push through, those issues will come forward in time of grief. Sadly, these unresolved issues, may bring a heavier resentment, causing overwhelming emotional reactions about time spent in the relationship, as opposed to focusing on the grief from the death and loss. One thing I have heard a lot is the comparison of being divorced and being a widow/widower. Being divorced is not the same as losing a spouse to death. Divorce is difficult and heartbreaking, however, the moving on and the sense of loss and recovery is very, very different. There is still a grieving process, however, it is a very different process.

Some things I went through in learning how to cope and move through my grief.

- Not sleeping well, maybe two to three hours at a time.
- Walking the floor to walk off scary or negative emotions.
- Dealing with the wee hours of the night when every thought can dump into your brain all at once or the loneliness really hits.

- That sudden fear of death for yourself
- Making plans to go somewhere that has been planned for a while, then all of a sudden cancelling them.
- Being overwhelmed with thoughts of the future and being alone.

It was startling to realize I didn't know how to work some of the things around my home, things that my spouse always took care of and that I just hadn't given much thought.

My husband handled everything with cars, yard, pipes and repairs. I handled everything within the house, cleaning, cooking, taking care of celebrations, dinners, gatherings and appointments.

The things that used to throw me off, make me mad, or cause frustration no longer received the same reaction as they once did. The biggest realization that helped was learning that the little things are just that, little things, and it hit me full on. What matters and what does not matter become magnified to the nth degree. Things that fall apart or break down do not cause the turmoil it once did. Things just get handled because nothing is as serious as dying!

Take pauses. Think things through. Breathe. Take mental breaks where you do not think of anything in particular. Take in your grief, shed tears you need to shed, laugh and cry over funny and sad memories. Come to terms with the regrets you may have for the things you did not do with or for your spouse, the things you left unsaid, the things said that did not need to be said, accept that we are human. Then let go, forgive yourself, forgive your spouse. Forgive and let go of all negative thoughts and memories, keep the lessons learned from those memories and thoughts but stop living within the negative world they bring. Keep ever present the fun, happy and beautiful memories, giving and allowing yourself freedom and permission to move forward.

What does moving forward mean? It means taking one step, one decision and making one choice at a time. And this may mean taking one second at a time, one minute at a time, one hour at a time, one day at a time, one week at a time, one month at a time, then one year at a time. It means sitting with grief and loss and allowing yourself to cry, be angry, be sad and be silent. It means talking about your losses and not talking about them. It means thinking about what we want and no longer want in our lives. All the parts of moving forward may run into opposition if there are adult children involved. This is when help from a grief counselor, coach or close friend may be needed. Many adult children do not want too much to change concerning the remaining parent.

EIGHT

Business Side of Grief

H ave you discussed what to do if something happens to
either person in a relationship, or a family member?

- Do each of you know how to run the household, indoor,
  outdoor, and financially?
- Does everyone have a will set in place and with whom?
  Without a will, even a simple one, it gets complicated as
  everything you own together does not automatically go to
  the surviving spouse only or chosen beneficiaries.
- Do each of you know the others end of life preferences?
- Is there a list of medications and the dosages needed?
- Are all important documents easy to locate such as:
- Life and medical Insurance policies. What are there
  instructions for activation upon illness or the death of
  either spouse?
- Marriage license, Birth Certificates, Passports, Military
  records (DD214), Retirement plans (401 K's)
- Medical (Doctors, hospitals of preference, it is helpful to
  have listed all surgeries, when and who did the surgery and
  medicines given)

- Papers for the purchase or sale of your home
- Names of utilities companies and whose name are the utilities in.
- About Social Security. If either spouse or both spouses are on Social Security, where are those papers? If both are on Social Security, the surviving spouse will receive the highest of the social security payments. Many people think the surviving spouse will receive both social security payments, which is not the case. My husband's social security payment was higher than mine therefore I received his payment and mine went away.
- Check all financial and bank records, look to see who the primary signer on all financial accounts is. What is the policy of the banks your accounts are in if a spouse passes away?
- Do you have a family accountant, if not who does the taxes, what deductions are taken and what paperwork is to be expected for doing the taxes?
- Who is called on for plumbing issues, furnace issues, water heater, garage door, for small home repairs, who does the lawn or in winter climates, who plows the snow? If there is a gas fireplace? Who should be called to come out and clean it?
- One of the biggest "Needs to Know" lists is passwords for all your records, computers, iPads, iPhones, programs, credit cards, bank accounts and all banking and taxes filed online. If each person does not want to share what passwords they use then write them down and put them in a sealed envelope and attach to your will or put them in a password protection app and only share the password to open that app to get to the rest of the passwords.
- Make a list of all automatic payments that is taken from your bank account or run against your credit cards. List the company, account the payment is taken from and the amount as well as the user I.D and password. These will

need to be canceled if they only pertained to the deceased spouse. When my husband passed away I had no idea he had so many automatic payments assigned to our credit cards. I had none of his user names or passwords to stop them until I canceled the credit cards.

- Where is the turn off valves for the water for the whole house should anything leak or a pipe break? Where is the turn off for the gas if you have a gas stove or fireplace.
- What is needed to winterize the home, car, snow blower, lawn mower? Because we lived in Alaska, we had a snow blower. I not only did not know how to work the new lawnmower, but the snow blower was huge, and I will unashamedly say I did not know how to run it either. These were never on my list of things to do therefore I had no reason, or so I thought, to bother with learning how to use them.
- I also learned, the hard way, not to allow anyone to mess with the electronic set up of my cable tv, music, and internet needs until I had time to figure out what I actually needed and what I did not need. I highly suggest that you do not allow someone who does not know the mechanics of how to connect all things electronic to try to change or make corrections to the system you have in place.

I must re-iterate, believe all those who have gone through this. Do NOT make any major decisions for a minimum of one year and better yet, not for at least 18 months. Of course, if there is no financial stability then this may have to be adjusted in order to live comfortably.

Our Stuff and Things

Life ends in an instant, without warning. Even when one is diagnosed with a terminal illness and given a timeline, the actual time of passing is still unknown. When the time does come that we take our last breath, it will feel like life was only a minuscule moment in time and we will be gone in an instant.

About a week after my husband passed away, I kept getting hit with the thoughts of how much the little things in life mattered. For most of my life I have been an avid reader and student of all things motivational, spiritual, positive thinking and the law of attraction teachings. I've read many books that teach about living in our now, and the reality of its meaning came crashing down on me in full blown awareness. I felt the full-on hit of the agony that comes in losing the opportunity to experience things we put off doing until other things or chores were done. The agony of time lost doing that which just spent our life minutes, and gave nothing back.

 I learned that all our "Stuff and Things" meant absolutely nothing in the end. All my life I have heard that you "can't take it with you", and now this very saying has become a truth that is staring me in the face as I looked at all of our "stuff and things" I still had.

There is no going back, no one more goodbyes, hellos or just because kisses. No one more hug, no one more "I love you" exchanged, no "Call me when you get to work," no "Call me when you leave work." No "Let's go to dinner tonight," no glass of wine waiting on the kitchen counter after work, no going to our son and daughter-in-law's home, together, to visit and to play with our grandchildren. No one more dinner together, no one more time to play and make love with each other. Everything my husband and I had thought and hoped we would do together came to a screeching halt, all brought about by the finality of death.

Selling the Home

Another huge decision was deciding what to do with our home. I researched what to expect as a widow, and what traps lie in waiting for a widow. One of the most important things that was consistently written was to not make any financial decisions for at least one year! My opinion is if finances are not in a critical place do not make any financial decisions for 18 months to two years. My way of thinking was very different at 18 months to two years than my thinking and how I felt was at the one-year mark. My financial consultant said, "Carolyn, at your age and stage of life, if you keep your home it could very well bleed whatever savings you have. Sell it and rent a nice condo or apartment, maybe rent in a nice retirement community." And as it happened, to sell my home I had to put a new roof on it and fix some plumbing and wiring. There were a lot of other reasons as well. My long-time neighbors who lived next to me and across from me, the ones I knew best and could count on for help, had also decided to pack it up and move to another state. We all had looked out for one another and I felt that my neighborhood protection system was leaving me, not to mention neighborhood friendships. My son and daughter-in-law came to me and suggested we "co-share expenses" since we both would be paying the same bills separately, and combining them would save all of us money. Although I always said that if anything happened to my husband I did not want to live with my children, going into a multigenerational living arrangement and sharing expenses sounded different and it allowed me to pay my own way. Of course, I am extremely grateful that my son, his beautiful wife and his daughters wanted me to be with them. I must also admit it sounded much better than living alone in some apartment in a neighborhood I did not know well.

In doing more research, I have found that we Americans are beginning to be better at watching out for our elderly parents and are not only more open about them living with us but are actually finding it financially helpful. This communal living is now called "Multigenerational living." If this is of interest to you and your family I suggest going online and researching Multigeneral Living and read everything posted on the subject. Most of the sites suggest questions to ask of each other so there are no surprises once everyone has moved in together. A couple sites I found very helpful were the reports from the Pew Research Center, and of course AARP. There are many websites that are offering reports and information on the art of multifamily living. Some of the things they all offered is the importance of having a family meeting before becoming a Multigenerational family and for everyone involved to lay all cards concerning likes, dislikes, needs and wants on the table. They also recommend having family meetings every couple months to see if anything has changed or needs to be adjusted. Many of the sites offer examples of the type of questions to ask of each family member who will be involved in this living arrangement. If you move with or close to your adult children it is important that you and your adult children have a conversation about expectations, needs, wants, what is convenient and what would not be convenient. Their lifestyle, values and rules and your lifestyle, values and rules will need to mesh, and many times that means several thoughtful compromises. Be very clear in everyone's discussions and opinions, including any children old enough to know what is about to happen. Even though we think we know each other well, we do not. As a parent we have a perception of who we think our adult children are and they have a perception of their own about who their parents are. Those perceptions can become a problem when reality is learned after moving in together. Therefore, those pre-move-in conversations are vital to success for all.

Many homeowners are remodeling their homes to include in-law suites also called mother-in-law suites. I also have noticed that several builders are now building the new homes specifically for multigenerational living opportunities. The building of the Tiny Homes has also revolutionized the opportunity for families to take part in Multigenerational living opportunities.

To quit or not to quit work

I have to say that if I could do it over, I would not have quit work as soon as I did. This is one of those decisions one should wait for at least one full year or maybe even two years to make, and I definitely should have waited to quit until my home actually sold. It

DEATH DID US PART

would have helped me get through the tough days and months that would lie ahead. However, since I had made the decision to sell my home and was not sure where I would be going as of yet, I decided to retire and take that vacation trip with my daughter-in-law and granddaughters before facing the process of having to get rid of 25 years of acquired "stuff and things" and sell my home of 25 years.

Leaving the state

The decision to leave the state after living in one place for 42 years was huge. There is so much to think about when considering making a giant leap of faith and moving to another state without your spouse.

- Are you moving where your children or extended family, parents, siblings, aunts/uncles/cousins' lives, as in "moving back home," or are you moving to be near a friend or friends? Are you moving with or to be with adult children for security of having backup care?
- Are you moving to a place you and your spouse always went for vacations? This is often easier as you are familiar with the surroundings and often already have friends living there.
- If you are retired or decide to retire and move, are you a joiner? Meaning, do you join groups easily, go to community centers, retirement communities, local libraries, senior centers, if you are old enough, to meet new friends and have an active life.
- When moving to another state, you will need to get a new driver's license, which may include taking a driver's written test.
- Are you unafraid, adventurous or daring in learning to get around or drive in new places and in a different state and city?
- Another crucial concern to get worked out is the handling

of your change of address notifications. This can be tricky if you do not have a specific address you are moving to.

- It is very helpful if you do a pre-move research for health care providers before you move. If possible try to get referrals from your existing health care providers such as;
- Doctor
- Dentist
- Optometrist
- Orthopedic Doctor
- Hospitals,
- Pharmacies
- Hairstylists, and Manicurists.
- Libraries, meeting facilities and if it pertains, Senior centers

You will also need to find your types of stores such as;

- Grocery stores
- Malls and clothing stores all of which may be new to you. Also, bear in mind that where ever you are moving to may not have your favorite shopping stores that you are used to.
- Have you considered the weather of the place you are choosing to move to? Do you want warm or hot all the time? Do you want four seasons, and what kind of terrain do you prefer, desert, lush greens, palm trees, oceans close, or forests and lakes? Are you contemplating being able to spend winter months in a warmer climate with other family or friends or hot summer months in cooler climates with family or friends? Living in Alaska we called those who once retired and lived summers in Alaska and winters in warmer climates, snowbirds. I also wish I had thought more about this option. I could easily be a snowbird, and for me it would have meant having the best of both worlds.

NINE

Our Fear of Death

F ear of death comes from the fear of the unknown and the will to exist longer on this earth, which is one of the reasons so many have a religious belief system. We want to believe our loved ones who have gone on before us are waiting on our path to the unknown to escort us to safety and our next forever life. We are also panicked at being no more!

The many belief systems of life after death are as varied as there are people. The underlying fear is astronomical. I absolutely cannot get my head around just not being here anymore.

Death is our biggest unknown, our biggest fear, the biggest reason we search for the 'why.'

The fear of death is one of the biggest reasons we don't have 'the discussions.' Many think if we don't talk about it, time will just keep marching on and we will continue as long as we think we should. If you're a believer of the Law of Attraction, the view that what we think about comes to fruition, then we must immediately stop our thoughts about death and dying.

We are so afraid of death that those dying or in hospice are often not given the chance to openly talk about how they are feeling about their life and how they have lived it, or to voice their fears of leaving this life. The big question of, "What do you want others to know about you, your thoughts, your life, advice to those you leave behind?" are seldom asked.

Many times, I have heard others say what they think a deceased loved one would have wanted for themselves or for those they are leaving behind, but what if we had actually asked them before they died? To ask them what they want us to know or do?

Many have said the following to me:

- "I am sure your husband would want you to move on"
- "I am sure if your husband could come back for a few minutes, he would tell you to live your life, to live it up as much as you can.
- "I just know your husband would want you to find someone else".
- "I am pretty sure your husband would want you to stay in your home.
- "I am sure your husband would not want you to stay alone.
- "I think your husband would want you to put in a security system or get a dog or a roommate.

Seriously, please, if you are tempted to say any of these things don't!

Time is no longer on my side and I am ever so aware of how important it is to stay in my Now. I can no longer put things I would love to do off for another day, because I have learned firsthand that another day may not come. I am grateful for every day I am gifted with, and I wish I had lived my whole life in a daily state of gratitude. It is so important to live our lives fulfilling our dreams, desires and intentions as if it was our last chance to do so. Tomorrow is not promised to us, but neither is the next second.

No one knows or is warned in a sudden death. I have often

wondered if my husband knew anything before he hit the ground. Did he have even a second to know this was going to be his time? Did he have even a second to think about his life, me, his children and his grandchildren?

The doctors said my husband died of a heart attack called "The Widow Maker" which means it was fast and final with one hit. We had so much more to do together. He was a devoted Papa to his granddaughters and talked about the stages of their lives he couldn't wait to give advice on.

The length of our life is a complete unknown, even if we are in the hospital, the doctor has said there is nothing more they can do and all the family has been called and are standing around the bed. Death will decide the time.

Many avoid important conversations with a person who has been told they are dying because everyone connected to this person is holding onto the hope that it will all change, and they will become the miracle we have heard of. We do not want to face the ending of their life and our lives without them in it. We may have never talked about the end of our life; therefore, we feel that at the time of the inevitable is certainly not the time to bring it up. Couples may have never talked about what either hope for their spouse if either one dies.

My husband always said that when his time came, he wanted me to move on and remarry right away. He was still old school and thought I needed to be taken care of. I used to tell our kids that if I went first, they should be understanding with their father as he was not a man who could be alone at all. I told them that, of course, he would not bring another woman to the funeral home, but he damn sure would have her waiting at the house. I told them it was alright with me and that if it was my time, I would not be returning, so in my belief system he needed to live as much and as fast as possible and remember only the good and fun times we had.

Some who have suffered a loss, or many losses, bring themselves personal destruction and harm to escape life without their loved one or loved ones. They drink heavily, overeat, do not ask for help if they feel depression has taken hold of them. They may take drugs to escape personal pains, overwhelming grief and the intensity of sadness that settles in their hearts and souls from losing someone they love and care for.

Many have not learned that forgiveness is the first steps to being able to bear the weight of grief. Most importantly forgiveness begins with forgiving ourselves for choices we have personally made or not made that has caused us anguish. We also need to grasp the fact that life just happens. We do our best at the time with whatever knowledge we have at the time.

When an elderly person brings up death or dying, others often panic or become fearful. They are told to not talk about that or don't worry about that right now. When an elderly person brings up death, they really need to or want to talk about it. Every birthday gives us less time on this earth and as we age, we become more and more aware of the time passing and we are more aware than ever that every morning we wake up is a gift, and every night we are grateful we made it another day.

Everyone is going to die. Better preparation for that time is needed for everyone's sake especially the ones who are left behind. The need to help our elderly prepare for their end of life wishes and to help those who will be left behind is becoming more and more acceptable and wanted. I have asked the surviving spouse of several terminal friends if they talked about the wants and needs with their dying loved one at any point of their life together. The answers are always no. I do caution that this is a personal judgement call by family members and the surviving spouse and the determination for this type of discussion is based on the mental and emotional state of the loved one who is dying. Hospice is often the bridge for this process.

If it is at all possible record conversations about their families, friends and life in general, especially if they tell their life stories. Ask them questions that will allow them to talk about their life, loves, and even their regrets. We used to have to hand write what an elderly person wanted to say to their loved ones but now with technology we can easily record what they have to say in their own voice.

I have read many versions of the 5, 10 or 25 things the dying want us to know. And they are all right on the money. The biggest issues are the regrets we have, of not living our lives to the fullest and not telling our loved ones how much they meant to us.

TEN

The Tough Conversations

M any of us are blessed to still have older family members with us. We visit and help them with some of their needs or just take them for a walk, to the store, parks, to visit other family, to visit their friends and some of us have become part-time or full-time caretakers.

What many of us have not had is that conversation with our loved ones about their life as they see it now. These are a few of the questions that need to be asked for the safety, security and respectfulness our elderly family members deserve;

- What and how do they want to be treated when physical limitations begin setting in?
- What do they want if they become incapacitated?
- What do they want to do or talk about if they become ill and know they do not have much longer to live?
- What are their wishes for their end of life ceremonies and belongings?
- Do they want a celebration of life after they have passed or before they pass? Yes, I said "before". In today's changing

times there are many who want a celebration of life while they are still able to communicate with those they love and have had long time friendships with. Hell, I am absolutely sure I want to be at my celebration of life, bring on the Margaritas, chocolate molten lava cakes and let's party and allow me to hug and visit with my family and friends. Then hopefully, I will peacefully and quietly go on to the next assignment that my maker has designed for me.

Many entertainers give their final goodbye tours for their fans and I think it is time we all go out as rock stars!!

If a parent has been widowed and has remarried or obtained a companion, what happens to their now spouse? Many adult children have a tough time with this one. They often feel that whatever was accumulated by their mother and father should remain as it was, and anyone new entering the picture gets nothing. This is not a very good or caring attitude for their remaining parent. Their parent has tried to continue to live their life and has moved through their own grief enough to bring another much-needed companion into their life. They and their new mate deserve the respect from their adult children. This is where emotions can run the gamut of hurt, anger, lack of understanding and selfishness, instead of love, understanding and an attitude of, "it is your life and we want you to be happy," and "we will do what is right for you and your now mate." Sadly, this is not the case for many. This doesn't even begin to touch on the issues of inheritance, properties and childhood homes that are difficult to let go of. Again, the widow or widower may need to bring in a grief counselor or coach, their pastor, if they have one, or a doctor who councils in grief to help everyone understand the process of moving through grief. I have a couple of very good friends in their senior years who have begrudged their very elderly parent of having a companion or new spouse. I ask them if they would prefer their parent to live alone and become a lonely sad person and surprisingly they could not answer these questions right away. Their hesitation was telling to say the least and I found a lot of sadness in their selfishness towards their parent. I have witnessed more families broken completely apart by inheritances, the distribution of existing properties and the remarriage of a widowed or widower parent. This is why communication between parents and children, especially older children, is so important. The need to respect an older parent's needs of having a companion in their life is tantamount to being understanding and loving about the loss they have experienced. It is important for the adult child to be supportive for them to move forward with their personal life. This works both ways, the widowed parent also needs to let their family know they are starting to see someone and not surprise their kids with a new mate out of the blue.

With many of my grief clients, I have found that women tend to grieve for what they had, while many men grieve for the future they will no longer have. The difference in grieving for what one had and grieving for what one no longer will have is two very different grief processes and often the grief is for the same loss. For instance, the loss of a child. The father of the child may turn his grieving inside, wanting to grieve privately, and he will want to remove the child's things from their room or he does not want the child's photos up for a while, while the mother of the child may want the child's photos around, she may want the child's room untouched, and she will want to talk about their child not only to her husband but to all who will listen.

Both are grieving and are doing their best to traverse the depths of hell as they maneuver through their loss. Neither is wrong in how they are handling their grief, and both should be given love, respect and understanding by their family and friends. Remember there is no right or wrong way to grieve a loss. I cannot say enough that grieving is a very personal emotion and must be allowed to take its course per the individual experiencing grief. Facing grief alone is a choice, there are many avenues of help when needed.

ELEVEN

The Secondary Losses

W ho gets it? Who does not?? These are questions that can only be answered one way. No one gets it unless they have experienced the loss of a mate, family member, friend or the numerous other losses that come to us in this lifetime.

Understand that once we have experienced these losses, we only "get it" and at best we can understand when another goes through the portals of shock, pain and grief. We do not know how another truly feels about their loss. We have all said to a new grieving widow, widower, parent, family member or friend that we are sorry for their loss and to please call us if there is anything we can do for them, then went home and carried on with our lives, never giving another thought to all that will be missed by the one or one's grieving.

When someone has lost a spouse they will soon be in a state called secondary grieving. This grieving also becomes harder in the second year of their loss. Below are just a few of the secondary losses I truly miss.

- Companionship
- Good morning hugs and kisses, goodbye kisses, I love you kisses and goodnight hugs and kisses
- Being able to watch the news and discuss and debate it
- Watching favorite movies and tv shows together
- Going to gatherings as a couple and being a couple
- Going shopping together even if it is just to a hardware store
- Having someone to have meals with, to cook with, trying a new recipe with,
- Taking a walk, holding hands and discussing life
- Going to the movies
- Going to our favorite restaurants just us two or meeting our friends
- Talking over current events and what our kids are up to along with gatherings we might want to attend
- Sitting on the deck or patio enjoying being together
- Traveling, vacationing and going for long rides together
- Having a drink together for no reason
- Scratching or having each other's backs, literally as well as figuratively
- Celebrating our anniversaries, and birthdays together, sometimes with family, sometimes with friends and many times just the two of us
- Annual holiday traditions and rituals
- Never worrying about the vehicles
- Never worrying that if car trouble happened, who would help me
- Getting several I love you and where did you put the _____? (fill in the blank) texts during the day.
- Having someone who always knows where we are for safety sake, like a text saying, "arrived safely at work," or a text saying "leaving work and stopping at the store."
- Missing shared and private jokes that would only make us laugh.

- I miss the snuggling, hugging, playing and private moments of intimacy, of which many seem hesitant to speak of. It seems as if no one wants to step up and say…. Yes, I miss the intimate times with my husband.

There are so many little things that cannot even be listed as the list would go on and on. Things that we do automatically and without thinking about as they have become habits. These come easily to a relationship, especially a long-term relationship, along with the knowledge we acquire like what each other likes to eat, to drink, what we have allergies to or how we do all sorts of things.

My husband and I, like many couples, had some really good times, some really bad times and everything in between in our life and marriage. We learned and grew from every shared experience, good or bad. We were born on the cusp of old-fashioned ways. I had enough "old fashioned ways" upbringing that we were able to compromise on many of our beliefs and preferences and somehow someway we made it all work. If we became broken we did what-ever we needed to do to fix us and our relationship.

TWELVE

Living an Aware Life

fter the shock of my husband's passing started to lessen, I knew that if he could come back for only a moment, he would remind me of our discussion that I needed to live my life to the fullest and that life needed to be lived now. I became so much more aware of the importance of our 'now.' Long before my husband died I read many of the books teaching about living in our 'now,' however, it took my husband's passing for the full-on reality of its meaning to come crashing down on me. I always thought I was living in the now. However, I realized that what I called living was more existing, doing my best to get through day by day, living for Fridays, the weekends and vacations.

When someone is in the midst of grief ask them about their needs, expectations and wants. Sit down with them and help them make a list of things that will need to get done along with bills that need to be paid and when. Look over the list and mark the things that others can do to help. Make a new list of things for the person grieving that they themselves needs to do and can do. Then make a new list of the things others can do and tell the grieving person that when someone asks them what they can do to help, hand them the list and allow them to pick that which they can accomplish for the griever. Give them a choice between spending time with them or helping them, as in, "I will come over Wednesday or Thursday and bring lunch and stay a while, which day would be preferable?" At the time of a person's loss, it is very busy with activity and everyone is around them. Most of the time the need for visits is from 3 or 6 months after their loss as by this time most everyone has returned to their own lives and schedules. It is also helpful to check on a person in grief throughout the first year as they will be going through all the "firsts" as in birthdays, anniversaries and holidays. Try to be with them on these emotional days.

There were some of these times I actually wanted to be alone, and others when I appreciated having my family and friends around to fill the day with the memories I so desperately wanted to talk about.

Often, someone who is grieving just wants to know the ones they lost are not forgotten.

As I come upon each of my loved ones 'Angelversaries' I make it a point to remember them for the joy they brought me not the death that took them. This in no way minimizes the ending of their life but helps to focus more on their living.

Be gentle, kind and understanding with yourself and anyone else who is going through grief. Shock, loss, pain and grief are, strangely enough, a part of living and experiencing life. Grief, in my experience, is the bridge to getting through the pain and sadness of loss. It may take work, but learning to use grief to help us move forward will also help us rebuild our life.

About the Author

Carolyn (Carrie) Schrader is a Certified Professional Life, NLP and Grief Coach. Carolyn's losses have been enormous. She has gone through the death of two beautiful children, her husband, grandparents, parents, aunts, uncles, cousins, siblings, many extended family members, friends and pets. She has also experienced personal health losses, jobs, homes, dreams, possibilities, relationships and at times the loss of who she was as a person. She has lived in Missouri, Washington, Oregon, Alaska, New Hampshire and now California. She grew up in a hardworking, blue collar family, learning about the tough times life can bring. Losses from her childhood taught her how to be a survivor.

Carolyn and her husband were blessed with twin sons, born in 1974. Due to a horrendous carbon monoxide accident, they died in 1976. In 1978 they were, once again, gifted with their third son who has blessed them with a daughter-in-law, and two granddaughters. Her husband of 46 years passed away in Alaska in 2014 and she continued to live in the state until 2016.

Carolyn enjoyed many careers in her over 50 years of work life. She held a License in Cosmetology for over 50 years, performed as a Radio Announcer (going on air with the moniker "Scout") with her husband, and worked as a Continuity Director, Copy Writer, and Radio Advertising sales for a number one country music morning show. Carolyn was in HR for many years as an Employment Counselor and Search Firm Recruiter. She has spent over 30 years working with most branches of the Military and their families serving as Office Manager and Deputy Director/Chief Financial Officer for the Armed Services YMCA of Alaska for ten years, where she also wrote a column in a military newspaper, called "Ask Mom", giving guidance to military and their families. Carolyn retired in 2014 as the Family Assistance Coordinator/Life Coach for the Alaska National Guard, a position she is very proud and humbled to have had. Carolyn has over 40 years as a Life Coach, using her skills, knowledge and trainings to help others.

Carolyn's greatest passion is helping others find their own positive life paths. To realize what a miracle they are and how much they have to offer this life they have been gifted with. To help everyone she comes in contact with to find the tools to help themselves obtain the goals they set and to maneuver through hardships and grief in order to live their best lives right where they are.

She holds an AA in Psychology, Certification for Professional Life, Grief and NLP Coaching, Grief Responder, Certified Crisis

Responder, Suicide Responder, Victims Advocate, and Certified Emergency Preparedness Trainer. Carolyn is an Author, Writer, Blogger, Published Columnist, Teacher/Trainer and Public Speaker.

carolynschrader.net
carolyn@carolynschrader.net

Notes

Notes

Notes

Notes

Notes

Notes

Notes

Notes

Made in the USA
Columbia, SC
16 September 2019